# Riding Right Young Rider's Workbook

A Guide to Horses, Barns, and the Fun of Riding

by

Andrea L. Beukema

Riding Right Farm

Buskirk, NY

Published by

Riding Right Farm

Hemstreet Farm, Inc.

334 County Route 59

Buskirk NY 12028

www.ridingfarm.com

Photography by Michael J. McNeil

## Acknowledgements

I would like to thank Sarah Bateman, Julia Houser, Kayla Irwin, and Adelle Woodcock for their help with the book's photography.

And of course, I'd like to thank Hollie McNeil for all of it.

# Table of Contents

# Part I: The Horse-Rider Partnership

To understand your horse, you have to think about what it's like to be a horse. If you are a horse, what makes you happy? What scares you?

Good riders understand their horses, to make it easier for horse and rider to work together. This section will help you to understand what your horse thinks about and how you can be a better partner with your horse.

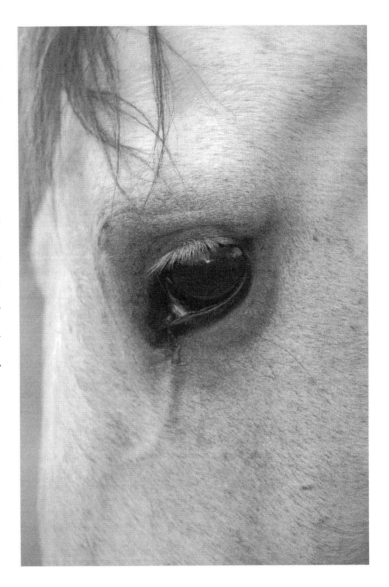

# Horses Are Herd Animals

Horses are herd animals. In the wild they're almost always in a group with other horses.

Being a part of a herd is safer, since horses take turns standing guard while others eat or rest. But it also means horses have to work with each other all the time. When you work with a horse, whether you are riding or just leading him, you become part of his herd.

**Question:**

Which horse is standing guard? How can you tell?

# Who's the Boss of That Herd?

Because a herd is a group, horses need a way to work together. There is always a 'boss' horse in every herd who takes the lead in deciding where they go and what they do.

The herd has a pecking order from the boss horse down to the bottom horse in the herd, based on how assertive the horses are with each other. Whenever a new horse is introduced to the herd, all of the horses have to work out where the new horse fits in. That's why you'll often see horses whinnying and even nipping at a new horse.

How can you tell who is the boss of a herd? The boss will be the horse who gets to eat first, or the one you see pushing other horses around. The boss will tell the other horses this by pinning their ears, kicking out and intimidating others away from their food or their space.

> **Words to Know:**
>
> Pecking order: How we describe the way animals know who is the boss and who gets bossed around.
>
> Pinning ears: When a horse points his ears backwards, flat to his neck.

> **Question:**
>
> How can you tell this horse is saying 'I'm the boss?'

3

# Horses Are Prey

Horses are prey. In the wild, they have to worry all the time about being eaten while they are trying to eat! Imagine trying to eat your breakfast while you're also keeping an eye out for wolves; that's what it's like for a wild horse.

In a herd, all of the horses are on the look-out for dangers. When one horse notices something that might be dangerous he will raise his head and perk up his ears. All of the other horses in the herd will notice this and start checking for danger themselves.

If the herd decides danger is approaching, they will run away as a group. And if they're attacked, the herd will work as a group to defend itself.

4

# All-Day Eaters

A horse's stomach is designed to constantly digest small amounts of grass. Most of a wild horse's day is spent eating grass with their herd. They graze for up to sixteen hours a day.

By eating all day, a horse can eat enough food but he's never too full to flee from danger.

Horses will take rests from eating. You might notice a horse lying down in the sunshine or playing with his friends, but before long they will return to grazing.

### Did You Know?

Horses can sleep while standing up, but for more restful sleep they will lie down.

### What is a Perfect Day for a Horse?

Write down what you think a perfect day for a horse would be. Hint – include LOTS of eating time.

7am: _____

9am: _____

11am: _____

1pm: _____

3pm: _____

5pm: _____

7pm: _____

9pm: _____

11pm: _____

# Fight or Flight

When a prey animal is feeling threatened, it will either attack the danger or run away. This is often called the 'fight or flight' response. 'Fight' means to attack the danger and 'flight' means to get away.

Because horses like to run away more than fight. When they sense danger they will usually gallop away. But if a horse is cornered or startled it will use it's hooves to kick at danger, rear up (so they look big and scary), or bite at the threat.

When you are with a horse in a small space – like a stall – it's important not to startle them, since you don't want them to feel threatened when they can't run away.

**Question:**

Which place in the pictures is more likely to worry your horse? Can you explain why?

# The Horse's Eyes

Because a horse is a prey animal, they need to see as much around them as possible. Horses' eyes are on the sides of their head, allowing them to see most of the way around their body. (Your eyes are in the front, so you can only see a bit less than half of the way around.)

A horse can't see directly behind himself. His butt gets in the way! That's why you shouldn't approach a horse from behind: since he can't see you coming, he might be startled.

A horse can see almost all the way around himself, but not behind him.

> **Did You Know?**
>
> A horse can use both eyes to look at the same thing - like humans do - or he can use each eye to look at different things, like a chameleon does!

# The Horse's Ears

Horses can move their ears around separately. This helps them figure out where a sound is coming from (and whether there is danger with that sound).

A horse's ears usually point toward something that is getting the horse's attention.

**Ears Pinned:** When a horse's ears are 'pinned' (back), he's worried or unhappy.

**Ears Up:** Happy or paying attention.

**One Ear Sideways:** Listening to something specific.

> **Question:**
> Which horse below has their ears pinned? Is listening to something in front? Listening to their left?

# A Horse's Touch

Horses have very sensitive skin and whiskers to help them feel things. A horse which weighs 1,200 pounds can feel a fly which weighs one hundred million times less!

The long whiskers that grow on a horse's muzzle and around their eyes are like a cat's whiskers. They're used to feel things close to their mouth or eyes.

Horses also use physical contact to communicate friendship. When one horse nibbles on the withers of another, they're being friendly. The withers are the only place a horse cannot itch using their own teeth or feet, so they will help each other out with a friendly wither scratching.

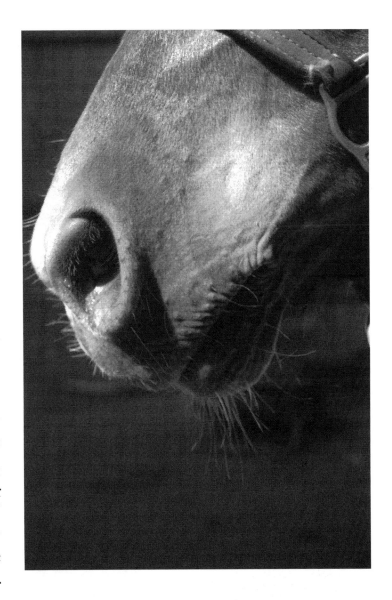

**Question:**

Do people use our sense of touch to communicate? Before you answer, think about getting a handshake or a hug.

# The Horse's Nose

Horses have a very good sense of smell. In the wild they would use this to smell an approaching predator.

Horses also use their sense of smell to greet each other and to know who's who in the herd. When you first meet a horse they will probably put their nose out to greet you and take a few deep breaths. This is their way of figuring out who you are.

Horses also use their nose to figure out who has been in their field. They will smell the manure (poops!) to see who has been there before them.

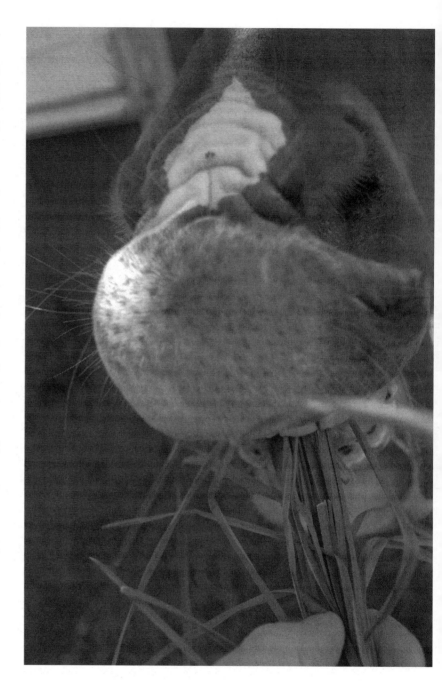

# Activity: Horse Sense

## Do People and Horses Use the Same Senses?

### Hearing:

How does a horse move their body when they want to hear something better or figure out where a sound is coming from? What would a person do if they heard a noise behind them?

### Touching:

Can you give an example of people using the sense of touch to say "hello" to each other? How can you touch a horse to say "hello" to him?

### Smell:

Can you think of a smell that makes you feel good or happy? What smells might make a horse happy?

### Sight:

Can you name something that you see that tells you about a danger? Can you think of something that a horse would see that would worry it?

# Part II: People as Partners With Horses

People and horses have been working as a team for thousands of years. Historians say that our culture would be very different without horses as part of our history.

For example, did you know that a group of people using horses has never lost a war to people who didn't use horses? Or that horses were the best way to grow food, since they could help you plow the fields? Or that horses let people travel long distances, making it possible to have large civilizations?

# Horses in History - Some Examples

**2000 BC:** People were riding horses in Mongolia, a part of Asia, more than 4000 years ago!

**860 BC:** People used horses as part of battles, the beginning of cavalry.

**175 AD:** Romans used horses for riding, to pull chariots, and for farming. There is a famous statue of the Roman Emperor Marcus Aurelius on horseback from this time.

**1700's:** Horses are used to pull fire wagons to fight fires in cities.

**1861:** The "Pony Express" was the fastest way to get mail across the United States. Riders carried the mail in relays across the Great Plains and Rocky Mountains.

## Did You Know?

Railroads are based on horse-drawn chariots? In Roman times, the wheels of Roman chariots were spaced about 4'9" apart. When the railroads started, they copied this same width, so that most modern railroads in the United States have rails which are almost the same width as a Roman Chariot.

When the first railroad locomotives were made, they were nicknamed "iron horses."

# Horses Today: Work and Fun

Although a few horses still have jobs, mostly they're used for fun. Here are some examples of both:

## Working Horses:

Police horses – horses that police use to patol where cars can't go, like parks and mountains.

Guide horses – miniature horses that do the same job as seeing-eye dogs, helping blind people.

## Fun Horses:

Sport horses – horses that are in competitions like dressage, jumping, etc.

Thoroughbreds – horses that run in races.

Trail horses – horses used to go on horseback hikes in the woods, etc.

## Horse Thinking:

For most horses, being with people and doing active things is fun, whether it's a police horse patrolling in a park or your horse trotting in the arena. It's the riders, not horses, who think some things are 'work' while others are 'play.'

# How Horses and Riders Work Together

Horses love to be with people who make them feel safe and take care of them. Horses love it when you spend time grooming, giving them plenty of hay and fresh water, and spending time just hanging out.

Most horses also love working with their rider, whether its being groomed, walking around the arena while you learn how to ride, or going for a long trail ride. Because horses are smart and a herd animal, they like working with a kind, attentive person.

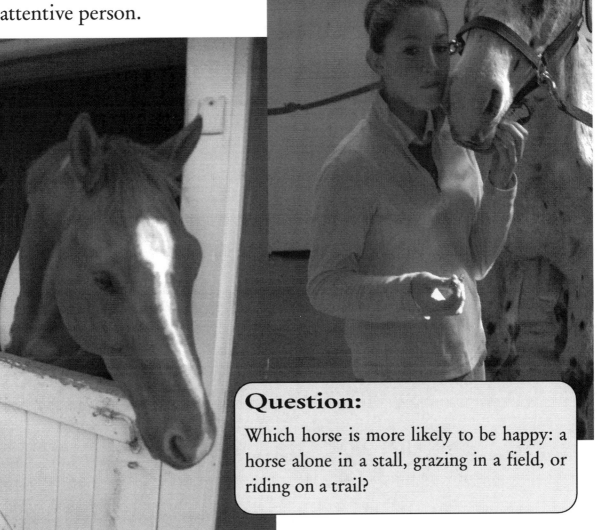

**Question:**

Which horse is more likely to be happy: a horse alone in a stall, grazing in a field, or riding on a trail?

# How Do You Become the Herd Boss?

When you are with your horse, part of your job is to be the herd boss. You want every horse to know you are a confident leader who will keep your herd safe. How do you do that?

**Movement & Body Language:** Walk calmly but with a purpose. Look where you are going and do not back up. The more space your body takes up, the more a horse will notice and pay attention to you. If you need to, get bigger by putting your arms up.

**Sound:** Talk to your horse using a calm, soft voice. If you are loud – even if it's because you're excited – horses might think something is wrong.

**Touch:** Use firm pressure and run your hand or brush in the direction the hair grows. A very light touch will feel more like you are tickling.

# Activity: Being the Boss

Look at the pictures below. Which rider is being confident with their horse? How can you tell from their body language?

**Words to Know:**

"Body Language" means the way you move your body and what it tells others about what you're feeling and thinking.

Horses are very sensitive to the body language of riders and other people around them.

# Part III: Describing Your Horse

As you learn to ride, it's important to be able to talk about horses correctly, so that other people in the barn or at a show know what you're talking about.

Since riding has some special words, it's like learning a small new language. For example, while you might call a horse 'brown,' horse people would call a horse 'chestnut' or 'bay,' depending on exactly which shade of brown it is.

# Horse Parts

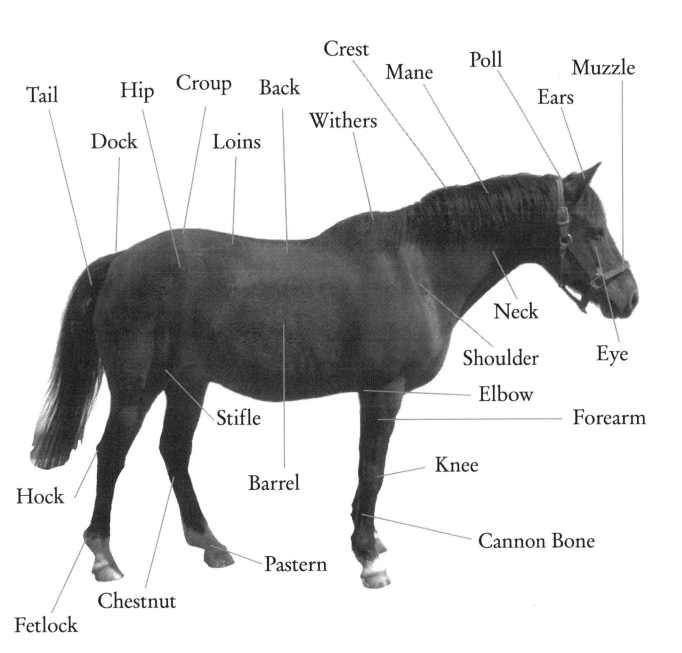

Tail · Hip · Croup · Back · Crest · Mane · Poll · Muzzle · Ears

Dock · Loins · Withers

Neck

Shoulder · Eye

Elbow

Forearm

Stifle

Knee

Hock · Barrel

Cannon Bone

Pastern

Chestnut

Fetlock

# Hoof Parts

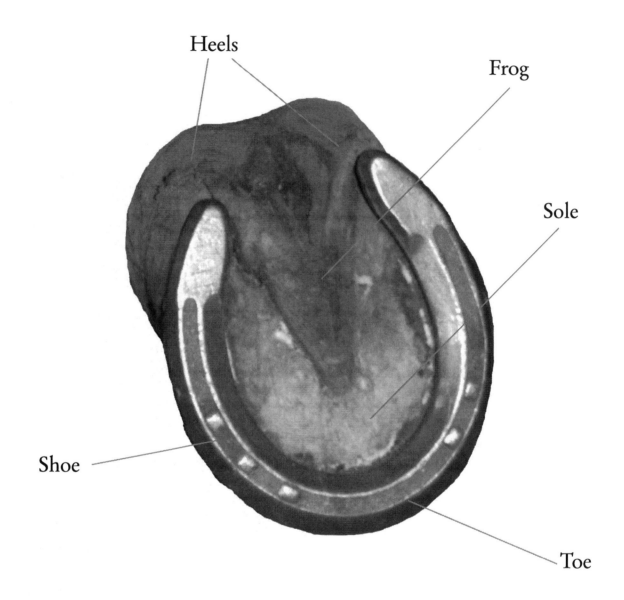

Heels

Frog

Sole

Shoe

Toe

## Did You Know?

The 'frog' is made of softer tissue than the rest of the hoof and helps pump blood back up the horse's leg towards their heart.

Every time a horse steps with their hoof the pressure helps squeeze the blood, like water squeezing out of a wet sneaker when people walk.

# Activity: Horse Parts and People Parts

Can you find the parts of a horse that are the same as a person? Some of them will surprise you.

Where is the head? Neck? Chest? Knee? Toe?

**Words to Know:**

Joints: Where two bones come together, making a body part bendable and moveable, like your fingers.

Skeleton: the bones that create a frame for the body of an animal.

# Measuring a Horse

How do you measure a horse?  There are a few differences between measuring people and measuring horses.

First, unlike people, horses are not measured from the gound to the top of their heads.  Horses are measured from the ground to the top of their withers.  The withers are the bony part at the bottom of the mane. (Look back at the 'horse parts' on page 19 if you're not sure.)

Second, people are ususaly measured in either feet and inches (in the United States) or meters (most of the rest of the world).  But horses are measured in 'hands.'

You'll probably never have to measure your horse - but if you do, you'll use a special ruler like the one in the picture below.

## What's a Hand?

When measuring a horse, a 'hand' is equal to four inches, which is approximately the width of an adult's hand.

People started measuring horses this way because it was easier than finding a ruler, then trying to get a horse to stand still.  And by measuring to the withers rather than the top of the head, it was measuring to a place most people could reach.

Plus the measurement wouldn't change every time a horse moved his head!

# Horse or Pony?

What's the difference between a horse and a pony? The most important difference is size: a pony is simply a small horse.

If a horse is fourteen hands and two inches tall (or less) at the withers, he's a pony; any bigger, and he's a horse. (Horse heights are written as hands and inches, so if a horse is "15.3" that means he's fifteen hands and three inches, too big to be a pony.)

**Activity: How Big Are You in Hands?**

Measure from the floor to the top of your shoulder (since people don't have withers, that's the best you can do). Measure yourself in 'hands', either using the width of an adult's real hand or using four inches for each hand.

Are you a horse or a pony? Are you 14.2 hands at your shoulder?

23

# Activity: How Big is Your Hand?

Measure your own hand along the edge of the page.

Is it exactly four inches wide? If it is, you're very lucky and very unusual. Most people have hands that are close to four inches, but not exactly that wide.

This is why we use measuring sticks and have set a "hand" to equal four inches. Imagine trying to tell how tall a horse really was if it measured 15 of your hands tall, but only 13 of your father's hands, that would be very confusing.

Four Inches = One Hand

# Horse and Pony Breeds

Just like there are different breeds of cats and dogs, there are different breeds of horses. And of course, the breeds of horses that are ususally smaller are known as pony breeds.

Usually, a horse (or pony) breed has typical colors, size, or temprament. For example, 'draft horses' are a series of breeds known for their large size, calm disposition, and the ability to pull lots of weight. 'Connemaras' are a breed from Ireland which are often light in color and smaller, pony-sized. But they can be mischevious.

When you are riding and especially if you ever want to have a horse or pony of your own, it's important to think about what breeds might fit your needs. Do you want a patient horse? A smart one? A horse that would be easy to take care of? Good for jumping? All these questions and many more should help you think about breeds.

American Paint Horse

German Riding Pony

# Colors

Horse colors have special names. Instead of just calling a horse 'brown,' horse people use particular words for particular shades.

Next time you're in a barn ask one of the instructors or an experienced rider to show you some of the examples of horses colors. Here are some of the 'horse color' names you'll hear about:

**Bay** horses are brown or dark reddish with black points.

**Chestnut** horses are light brown with points the same color.

**Black** horses are all black - without any brown or other colors mixed in.

**Grey** horses come in many shades, ranging from nearly black to mostly white, but with black skin under their hair.

**Paint** horses usually have big areas of solid colors, like a cow. **Skewbald** is a kind of paint with white and other non-black patches. **Piebald** horses are black and white.

**Appaloosas** are speckled or have dalmatian-like spots on top of many different colors.

> ## Words to Know:
>
> "Points" are the ends of a horse's legs, the tips of the ears, the mane, and the tail. On most horses the points are all approximately the same color.
>
> "Whorls" are the patterns made by the hair on a horse, like a "cow-lick."

# Face Markings

Another way to describe a horse is by his markings. Somebody might ask you to get a horse from a pasture by saying "he's the bay horse with the white blaze." Some of the common face markings are:

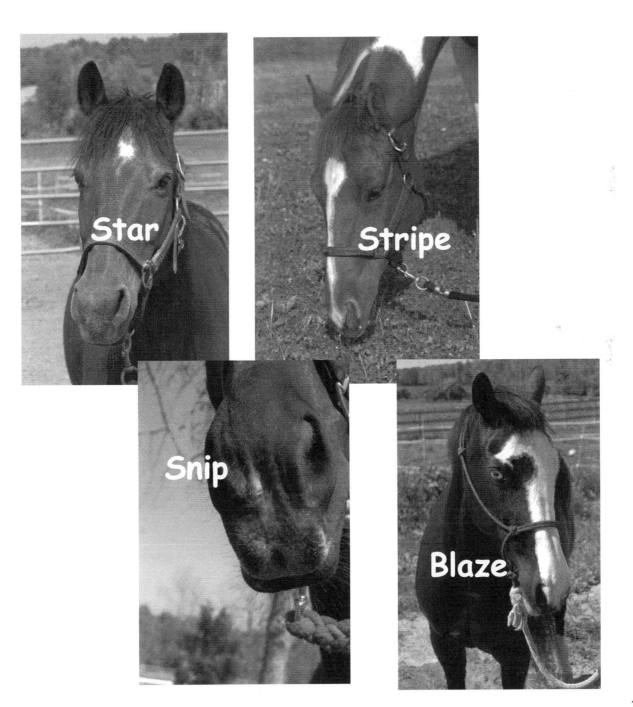

Star

Stripe

Snip

Blaze

# Leg Markings

In additon to colors and face markings, riders also use leg markings to describe a horse. Here are four of the most common ones:

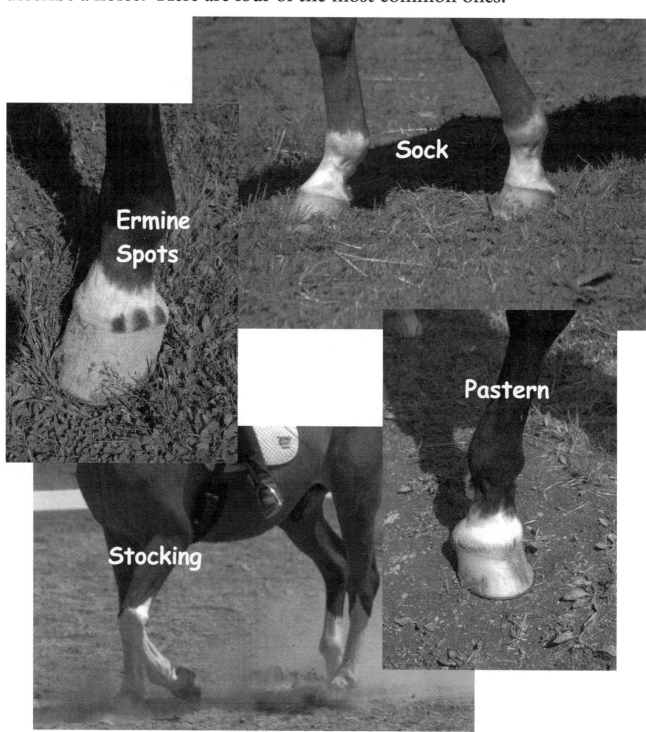

# Activity: Match the Horse

Look at the pictures below. Which horse is the black horse with a blaze and socks on the hind legs? Which is the bay horse with four white pasterns and a star? Which is the paint horse?

# Part IV: Getting Ready to Ride

When you ride, you need to wear the right clothes and have the right equipment. This makes your riding both more safe and more fun.

# Helmet

**A helmet is the most important part of your riding gear.** Always wear a helmet when working around horses and riding. Even if a horse just accidentally bumps his head against yours, you can get hurt because the horse is so much bigger than you.

The helmet needs to be made for riding, not a bike helmet, hockey helmet, top hat or baseball cap! A safe helmet will have a sticker inside that says it has been certified by the ASTM and SEI. It is also important that your riding helmet is not too old – the rule of thumb is that helmets need to be replaced every 5 years.

No!

## Does your helmet fit?

Do your eyebrows wiggle when you jiggle the brim? If the helmet is snug, the answer should be yes. But the helmet shouldn't be too tight. If it feels like your brain is going to be squished out your ears, that's too tight.

And the chin strap must be snugly fastened, too.

# Dressed to Ride

What should you wear to ride?  You don't need formal 'show clothes' to be a rider, just a few practical things to wear:

Start with a riding helmet on your head.

You should wear a comfortable shirt, one that lets your hands, arms, and body move freely.

Gloves are nice, but not required.  If you do use them, get ones with rubber or leather grips.

You don't need to wear riding breeches or jodhpurs at the beginning, but something soft and stretchy like leggings will be more comfortable than jeans.

Boots protect your feet and help keep your foot in the stirrup.  They should have a closed toe, a flat sole and a small heel to keep your foot from sliding through your stirrup iron. 'Paddock boots' are boots made for wearing around the barn and while riding.

# Riding in Extreme Weather

## Riding in the cold:

Bundle up the same way you would for sledding or skiing. It's OK to wear Winter boots (if they're safe in the stirrups - ask your instructor), gloves and snow pants. Helmet covers, neck warmers and long johns will help you stay warm too.

## Riding in the heat:

Stay cool by wearing a lightweight tee shirt and by using a helmet with lots of air holes. You might be tempted to try riding in shorts, but this is not a good idea; you will end up with pinched thighs and rubbed legs. Sneakers and sandals are also dangerous around a barn. Your feet are best protected when they are in paddock boots.

# Activity: Dressed to Ride

Which clothing in this pile of pictures is good for riding? Which is not? Why?

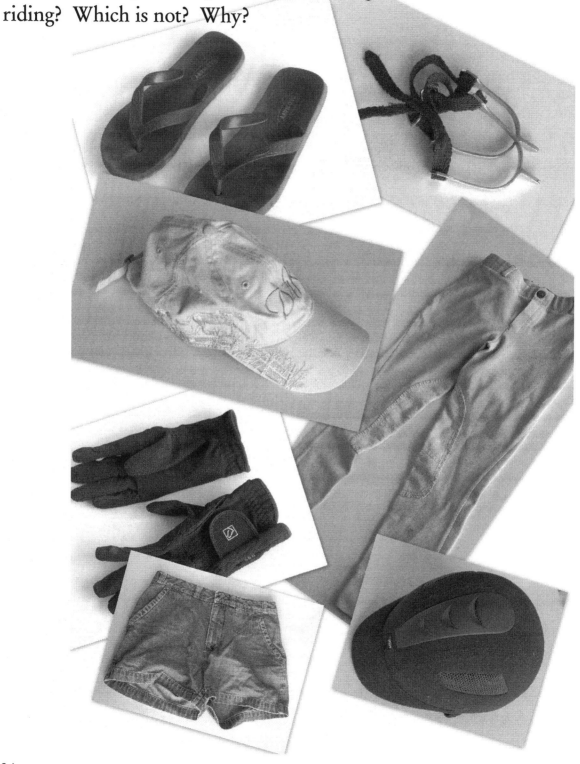

# Part V: Arriving at the Barn

Once you arrive at the barn, there are a few things to do before you can get on your horse and ride. Plus there's the need to be thoughtful of other horses and riders.

This section will help you with all that.

# Manners and Safety Around the Farm

A barn is a safer, more fun place to be if everyone tries to be considerate of each other. Here are a few ways you can do that for you and your horse:

• Horses like calm people better than noisy, rowdy ones. When you're around the barn, talk in a normal voice and don't shout.

• Slow is also better than fast. Even if you're excited, it's better to walk in a barn than run.

• Being on-time is thoughtful for both your horse and your instructor. Being late and making your horse wait for you is boring for the horse. You should be at the barn at least 20 minutes before your lesson.

• In the barn, horses come first. That means if you're walking, make sure there's room for horses to get past you easily. That's true whether the horse is being ridden or being walked from the ground.

• Don't spook horses (see p. 41), especially by walking up behind them. If you can't see the horse's eye clearly, he can't see you.

• Stay out of the 'kick area' behind a horse. If they get scared and kick out, you want to be somewhere else!

### Did You Know?

If you see a horse with a red ribbon in its tail at a show, that's a warning that the horse is likely to kick.

Give those horses extra room behind!

# The Busy Barn

Barns are often busy places and will have tractors, golf carts, and other things moving around.

Vets, farriers, and barn workers all have a job to do, and you can learn a lot about horses and riding from them. If you want to watch, just ask. Most of them will be happy to help you learn.

**Activity:**

Taking care of horses takes lots of work. How many tasks can you list? Here are some hints: Who feeds the horses? Cleans the stalls? Keeps them healthy? Checks their feet? Checks their teeth? Fixes fences and broken stalls? Harvests the hay? Mixes the grain?

# Who Are You Riding?

One of the first jobs for you when you arrive at the barn is to find out which horse you are riding. Most barns will post this in a convenient location, such as a chalkboard or clipboard.

In most barns, you'll end up riding one horse more often than the others. Your instructor will think about a good match between you and the horses at the farm, and will have you ride the one they think is best for you most of the time.

Sometimes they'll pick a horse that isn't your regular, familiar one - don't be disappointed. Maybe it's because that horse is sick, tired, or needs a day off. Or maybe it's because the instructor thinks a different horse can do a better job of teaching you. You will learn a lot by riding many different horses and ponies.

## Activity:

Can you think of five things which would make a horse one of your favorites? Can you think of five reasons your instructor might have you ride a horse which isn't your favorite?

# Part VI: Getting Your Horse Ready

When you're getting ready for school, you need to make sure you have the things you need before you go. Books? Lunch? Paper? Pencils?

Riding your horse is like that, too. Before you can get on and ride, you need to make sure your horse is ready by grooming him and putting on his tack. (Not sure what 'tack' means? Don't worry, you'll find out soon!)

# Putting on a Halter

First things first: make sure you're wearing a helmet before you start working with horses!

Confidently approach your horse by walking toward their shoulder. Remember to walk towards them where they can see you, and say hello when you get close so they aren't startled by you.

Then, put the lead rope over their neck.

Next, slip the halter over their nose.

Last, either buckle the halter behind the ears (of the horse, not your ears, silly!) or hook the throat strap depending on the style of halter you use.

When you're done, it should look like the picture.

# Leading a Horse

To lead your horse, stand on your horse's left side, hold the lead rope in both hands and walk forward.

Stay between your horse's eye and shoulder.

A gentle tug of the rope may be needed to stop, although a well trained horse should stop when you do.

Watch Out! If you get too close or in front of your horse, you could be stepped on.

Hold the rope in your right hand, with the extra rope in your left. Never wrap the rope around your hand, since you could get tangled and dragged if the horse spooks.

> **Words to Know:**
>
> "Spook" is the word for when a horse is scared by something which surprises him and it makes him move suddenly.

# Misbehaving Ponies

Sometimes horses and ponies are naughty! Ponies, especially, have a reputation for mischief and trouble.

Here are some of the things horses and ponies often do wrong and why they do it:

**Drag you to food:** Ponies love food. Once a pony has succeded in dragging you to food, they will likely try it again, so try to stop them right at the start. If a pony is really strong, ask for help leading them.

**Step on your toes:** This isn't really the pony's fault. Because ponies can't see directly below their nose, they can't see your feet if you are walking or standing too close to them.

**Make faces or bite:** Ponies might not like another horse in their space, or they might not like their girth being tightened. If a pony senses that you are afraid or intimidated, they might try be the herd boss of you.

**Fidget and fuss:** If your pony is bored, they might start to fidget. Other times, a pony is moving to scratch an itch or get at a bug that's bugging them! Really tricky ponies will toss their head at the exact moment you are trying to put the bit into their mouth or buckle the noseband.

# Activity: Leading a Horse Correctly

**Find the Mistakes:**

Can you find the mistakes this rider is making while leading her pony?

# Tying a Horse

It's important to tie your horse whenever you want to work with or around them.

If your horse isn't tied when you're working on him, he could turn and step on you. If you are working in a stall or in the barn and don't tie your horse, your horse could get loose.

Most farms have cross ties where you can groom and tack up your horse. When using cross ties, make sure you have one attached to each side of the halter.

If you don't have cross ties you can use a quick release knot – learn how to tie one on the next page.

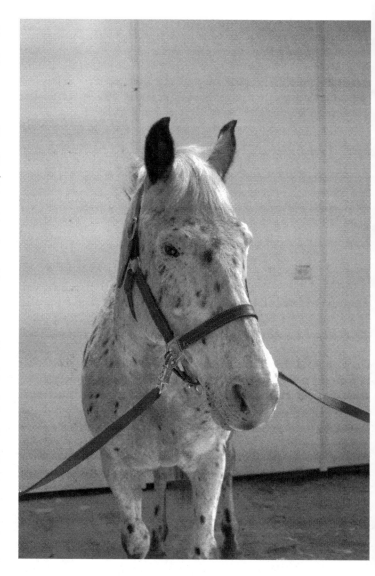

# Tying a Quick Release Knot

1 - Always start with a loop of twine or other breakable material. It's important that a horse can break free if they are struggling. Otherwise, they can hurt themselves.

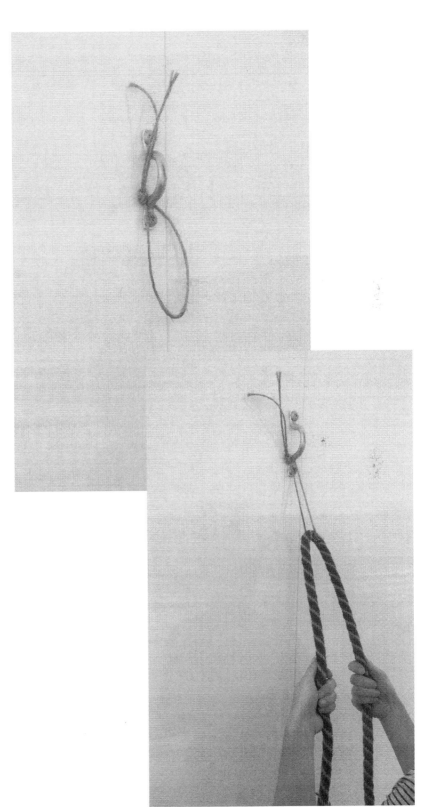

2 - Pull the lead rope through the loop of twine. Make sure the distance between the loop and the horse's halter is short enough that the horse can't step on the lead rope.

3 - Make a loop with the part of the lead rope which is opposite the snap.

4 - Make a new loop from the same end of the rope, and pass the second loop through the first one.

5 - Push the first loop of the rope up to the twine loop to tighten eveything up. The second loop should end up loose and the first loop should be snug. If it's right, pulling on the non-snap end will untie the rope.

# Where Should You Tie Your Horse?

When tying your horse, think about the safety of your horse, people in the area, and other horses. Here are some examples of good and bad places:

**Good:** Tie rings in a barn. Barns will usually built-in ties for horses which should include a break-away part, such as bailing twine.

**Bad:** A board on a fence. Since a horse is strong enough to pull the board off the fence, and there will be nails in the board, that would be dangerous to him.

**Good:** A fence post. A good, strong fence post won't come out of the gound, so this is usually a safe choice.

**Bad:** Another horse, your dog, or your little brother.

**Good:** Bailing twine around a sturdy metal stall bar.

NO!

## Important to Know:

When you tie a horse, make sure either the halter or the tie or will break if the horse gets scared. A leather halter, a nylon halter with a leather break-away piece, or a tie which is attached to some bailing twine are all safe. A nylon halter and rope tied directly to the wall is not, since the horse can pull and hurt themselves.

# Taking Off a Blanket

If your horse is wearing a blanket, take it off.

Start by unhooking the straps that go around the hind legs.

Then unhook the belly straps.

Next, un-buckle the blanket at the chest.

Finally, you can slide the blanket off from the side of your horse.

To put the blanket back on work in reverse order.

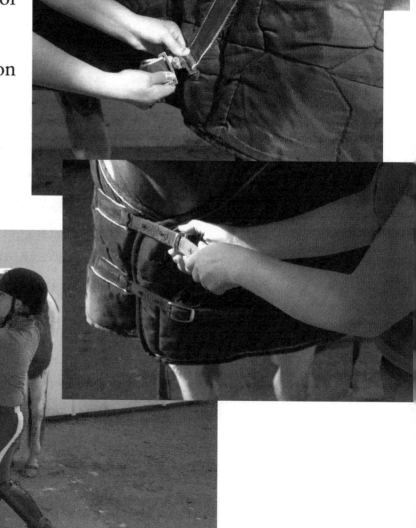

# Grooming Tools

What Are the Basic Horse Gooming Tools?  What Are They Used For?

### Curry Comb

Gets dried mud and shedding fur loosened up.

### Hard Brush

Removes all the dirt and loose hair.

### Soft Brush

Cleans dirt and dust away from sensitive eyes and ears, make's your horse's whole body shine.

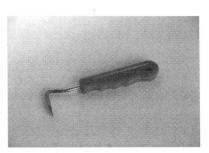

### Hoof Pick

Removes stones that could hurt your horse's feet, and prevents horses from developing thrush, a bacteria that will grow in dirty hooves.

# Steps in Grooming

## Grooming Steps:

### 1. Pick the Horse's Feet:

Tool: Hoof Pick

Dig in and carefully work from heel to toe (skipping the frog - see p. 20) cleaning out mud, bedding and any stones that get stuck in your horses feet.

### 2. Curry your horses body:

Tool: Curry Comb

Work from neck to tail pressing firmly making big circular motions over your horses neck, back, belly and rump. But skip the bony parts of the horse, including the face and legs.

### 3. Brush off the loose mud and fur:

Tool: Hard Brush – sometimes called a dandy brush

Working from neck to tail flick the brush in the direction the hair grows brushing away all the mud, dust and fur that you loosened with the curry comb

# 4. Brush your horse's face and legs, and add a final shine to their body.

Tool: Soft Brush – sometimes called a body brush

Carefully brush around your horses eyes and ears, and down their legs. These are all places where your horse's bones are closer to their skin so you want to be gentle.  After doing the legs and face, you can run the soft brush over their whole body to remove any stray bits of dust.

# Activity: Grooming

Can you match the correct grooming tool with the parts of the horse that need grooming?

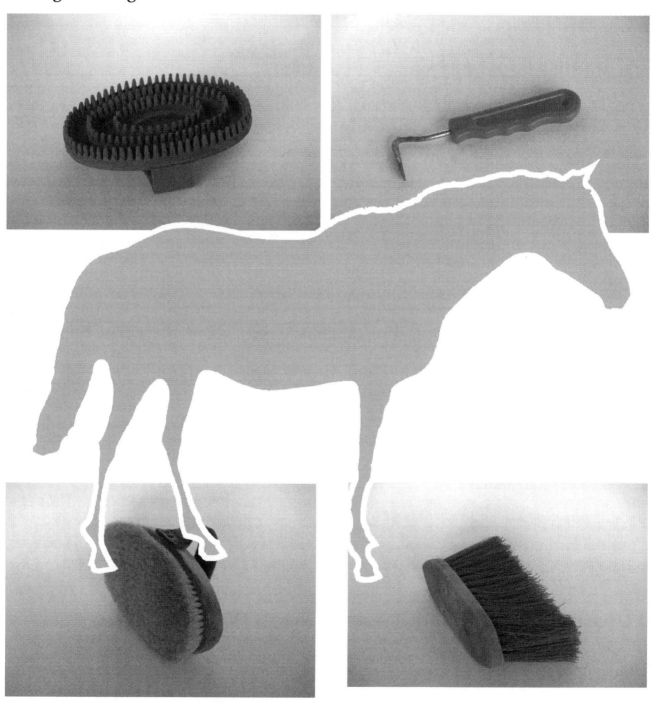

# Tacking Up - Gather the Equipment

Once you've groomed your horse, you are ready to tack up. Head into the tack room of your barn and gather up all the parts you'll need, typically the following:

**Saddle Pad:** a soft fabric pad which goes on your horse's back

**Lift Pad:** some horses - especially older ones - use a lift pad, a foam pad which goes between the saddle pad and the saddle. These pads are also called 'risers' or 'lollypop pads.'

**Saddle:** the place where you sit!

**Girth:** a band of leather, cloth, or sometimes woven rope which goes under the horse's belly to hold the saddle on.

**Bridle:** the straps which fit over the horse's head, holds the bit in the horse's mouth and has the reins attached.

# Saddle Parts

Before you ride, you should know the parts of the saddle and what they do.

Stirrup Bar

(holds stirrup leather)

Pommel

Cantle

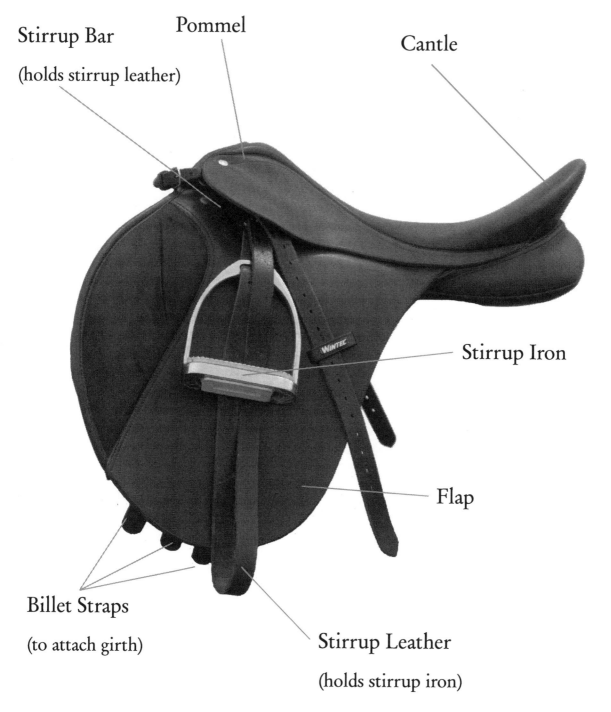

Stirrup Iron

Flap

Billet Straps

(to attach girth)

Stirrup Leather

(holds stirrup iron)

# Bridle Parts

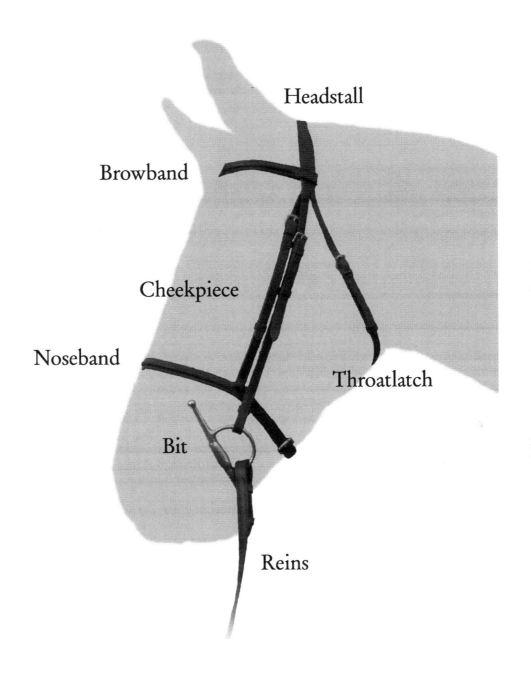

Headstall

Browband

Cheekpiece

Noseband

Throatlatch

Bit

Reins

# Activity: Tacking Up

Here's a bunch of things you'll find around a barn. Which of them are used for tacking up your horse?

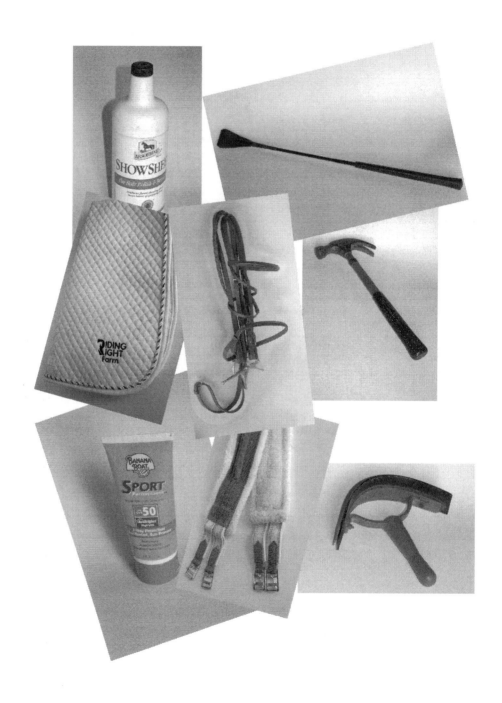

# Tacking Up - Putting on the Saddle

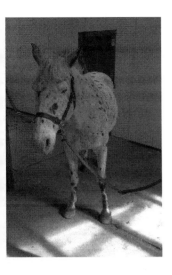

It's time to put on the saddle!

(1) Have your horse standing on cross ties or tied with a quick release knot.

**Don't Forget:**

A helmet for your head is part of tacking up. Always be safe!

(2) Start by putting your saddle pad on the horse's back. Put it a little too far forward at first, so as you slide it back into place you are also smoothing out the hair underneath. Your saddle pad should cover the horse's withers. If your horse uses a lift pad, put it on next.

(3) Then, put your saddle on top of the saddle pad (or lift pad). Make sure you have about two inches of saddle pad sticking out in front of your saddle.

(4) The most important piece is your girth – it holds your saddle on your horse! Some horses are 'girthy,' which means they do not like their girth being tightened and will bite or kick out, so be careful and ask for help if you are not sure how a horse behaves. Leave the girth a little loose while you are tacking up; you will tighten it more before you get on your horse.

# Tacking Up - Putting on the Bridle

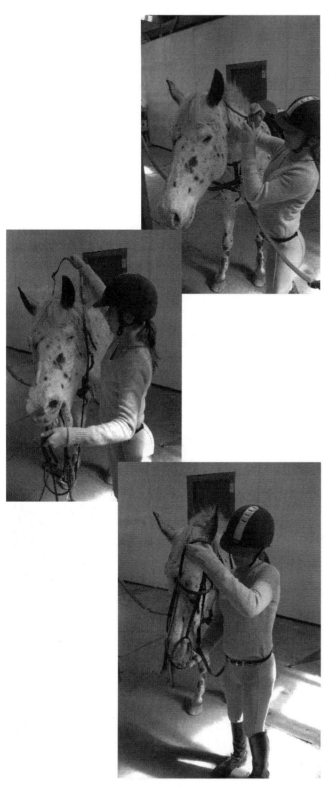

After your saddle is on you can put on your horse's bridle.

(1) Start by taking the halter off their head, and buckling it around their neck – this frees their head for you but your horse is still tied so they can't wander off.

(2) Next put the reins over the horse's neck

(3) Putting the bit in the mouth is sometimes tricky – have a step stool to stand on if you can't reach your horse's ears. While holding the bridle in your right hand, use your left hand to guide the bit into the horse's mouth. You might need to stick your thumb into the corner of the mouth to get them to open their mouth.

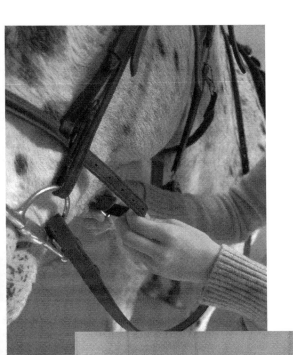

(4) Once you have the bit in the mouth, slide the headstall over your horse's ear.

(5) Fasten the buckles. Fasten the throatlatch so one hand or fist will fit between the strap and your horse. Fasten the noseband snugly around the nose, checking that you are running the noseband straps under the cheek pieces.

# Part VII: Getting On Your Horse. And Off.

You've dressed correctly, groomed your horse, put on his tack, and now you're ready to get on! Plus you need how to get off, too.

# Leading With Reins

Now it's time to lead your horse to the arena or other space where you will be riding. When you lead your horse with reins, you should take the reins off the horse's neck and hold them in both hands. Don't forget to lead from the left side of the horse!

You should also make sure that your stirrup irons are 'run up,' which means sliding them up to the top of the stirrup leathers, then tucking the leathers through the stirrups. It sounds tricky, but it's easy once you see how.

**Words to Know:**

The stirrups to the right are 'run up', making them safer for horse and handler when leading the horse.

# Equipment & Safety Check

Just like a pilot checking the airplane before they take off, you should do a quick safety check on your horse and equipment before you get on. Have an instructor or adult help you check your equipment.

## Rider Checks:

Helmet:  Is it snug and is the chin strap buckled?

Shoes or boots:  Are they safe, with a small heel?

Gum: Got gum?  Make it gone!

Jewelry:  Take off any jewelry that dangles or could get caught.

## Horse Checks:

Bridle:  Buckled at the noseband and throatlatch?  Reins ready?

Girth: Check to make sure it's tight.  Some ponies hold their breath and puff out their sides, so you might have to tighten the girth a hole or two, walk forward and then tighten the girth again.

Stirrups:  Pull down your stirrup irons and check their length.

## Smart Trick:

To estimate the correct length for your stirrups, put your fingertips on the stirrup bar (on the saddle), then put the stirrup iron into your arm pit. If the bottom of the iron just touches your body, your stirrups are probably close to correct.

# Mounting - How to Get On

Lead your horse to the mounting block. The block should be on your horse's left.

Put your left foot into the stirrup iron, swing your right leg over the back of the saddle, and gently settle into the seat.

Your instructor can help you adjust your stirrup irons.

## Why the Left Side of the Horse?

We mount from the left and swing our right leg over the back of the horse because knights and even earlier horse-warriors always carried their swords on their left hip.

# Getting Comfortable

Hooray you made it onto your horse! The first thing you should do is get off. Really!

Part of being confident **on** your horse is being confident about getting **off** your horse. So one of the very first things you should practice is dismounting.

This is especially true if you feel a bit nervous. If you know how to get off correctly, you'll feel better about being in the saddle.

# Dismounting

You are going to swing off of your horse's left side. Why the left side? If you don't know the answer, you skipped a page! And if you do know the answer, give yourself a gold star.

1. Take both feet out of your stirrups.

2. Swing your right leg over the back of the saddle. Try to touch your belly to the pommel of the saddle, since this will make it easier.

3. Slide down to the ground with your stomach facing your horse. Imagine your horse is a big slide, and have fun!

4. Land on your feet. (But don't worry if you fall on your butt the first few times.)

# Part VIII: Riding - First Lessons

Now you know how to think like a horse, lead a horse, tack up a horse, and even get on and off a horse. It's time to ride.

In the beginning, you will often be working one-on-one with an instructor leading while you develop the comfort and balance that are needed before you can be on your own. After you have spent time on the lead line or lunge line (two ways for your instructor to guide your horse while you ride) you will be ready to take up the reins and learn how to ask your pony to walk forward, stop and turn.

# Sitting in Balance

Settle into your saddle and let your legs hang relaxed.

You want to have a straight line from your head through your shoulder, hip and foot.

Let your arms hang loosely down. Imagine you are standing on the ground without the horse. Your riding position should be more like standing than sitting!

## Smart Trick:

To see if your riding position is correct, imagine your pony suddenly, magically disappearing. Would you land on your feet? If the answer is 'yes', you're position is good. Look at the two riders on the left to see the difference.

# Finding Your Feet

Put your feet into the stirrup irons. You want to put the stirrups under the balls of your feet (just behind your toes).

An important part of riding is having a good feeling for where your feet are and what they are doing. Here are a few things you can do to work on that:

**Try This:**

Can you take your feet out of the stirrups and then put them back in without looking at your feet?

Can you take your feet out of the irons and pick them back up? Can you stand up? Can you smoothly sit down?

Sitting down takes leg strength and coordination. At first it might feel like you are landing on your saddle with a thud. But keep practicing until you can do it smoothly.

# Balance While Moving

To be a good rider you need to stay in balance with a moving horse.  This is being a "good backpack" for your horse.

As your instructor leads your horse with you sitting tall in the saddle, allow your body to move with the horse.  Let your arms hang freely by your sides or hold on to the pommel of your saddle.  Don't worry about the reins for now.

Do you feel relaxed?  Imagine your joints are made out of Jello so that each step your horse takes makes you a little jiggly, just like Jello.

# Holding the Reins

Your balance and your feet are actually more important in riding than your hands and reins, but that doesn't mean you can skip learning about the reins.

To hold the reins correctly, scoop up the reins with your three middle-most fingers and make a fist around the rein, with your thumb on top. The rein should make a straight line from your elbow to your hand to the horse's mouth.

**Lengthening and shortening the reins:**

'Shorter' is holding the reins closer to your horse's mouth, so that the distance between your hand and the horse's mouth is shorter. Longer is just the opposite.

How do you make your reins shorter? Pinch the rein with the opposite hand and slide your hand closer to the horse's mouth.

How do you make your reins longer?

Open your fingers a little and allow the reins to slowly slide through.

# Activity: Good Reins

Whose reins are too long?  Whose reins are too long?

Whose reins look just right for walking around the arena?

# Correct, Balanced Position

This picture shows a rider who is ready to go. This is a 'correct, balanced position' that will help you use the correct aids and stay balanced as you learn how to ride. Notice the straight line from her head through her shoulder, hip and heel. There is a second straight line running from her elbow through her hand and to the corner of the horses mouth. Imagine this horse disappearing. Would she land on her feet?

Check your position and balance before you move on:

• Both feet in the stirrups with your heels sinking lower than your toes.

• Sitting in balance, not leaning off to one side or slouching.

• Reins in both hands with fingers closed and thumbs on top.

• And finally, do you feel comfortable moving with a horse as they are led around at the walk?

Now you can learn how to ask your horse to do things like walk forward, stop, turn and trot.

# Have a Plan

Most of the time, horses want to make their riders happy by doing what their riders ask. But what happens if the rider isn't sure? It just confuses both you and your horse.

When you are on your horse, it's your job to have a basic plan for what you're going to do. Do you want to have your horse stand still? Walk forward? Turn left?

Before you can ask you horse to do something, you have to decide what you want him to do.

# Talk to Your Horse: Use Aids

When you learn to ride, a big part of your job is learning to tell your horse what you want him to do. Since horses don't understand English, you need to learn a new way of communicating with your horse: aids.

'Aids' is the word riders use for the ways they communicate with their horse. There are four main types of aids:

**Weight and Seat Aids:** When you shift your weight to one side or the other, your horse feels that, and will use that to figure out what you want him to do. For example, when you look to the left, you body shifts and your horse feels it.

**Leg Aids:** When you squeeze, tap, or move your leg, that's another thing the horse feels and uses to know what you want.

**Hand or Rein Aids:** The reins are also a way to 'talk' to your horse. When you squeeze or loosen your reins, you're telling you horse where you want to go, or how fast they should be going.

**Additional Aids:** There are other aids, too, like your voice, a crop, etc. But the seat, legs, and hands are the most important, and the ones you'll want to learn first.

# Go and Whoa - Start and Stop

The simplest two things you can say to your horse are 'go' and 'whoa.'

So one of the first things you'll want to know is how get those messages to your horse: 'go' is a quick tap of the legs and 'whoa' is a gentle squeeze on both reins.

## Go:

To ask your horse to go, give him a quick tap of your legs. Different horses will need more or less of a tap, but start out being gentle. If he doesn't listen, you can give him a stronger second tap.

## Whoa:

To ask your horse to stop, sit deep in the saddle and give him a short squeeze with your reins. Remember that the reins are connected to the horse's mouth, so be soft and gentle.

# Steering

You steer your horse with your reins - but that's only part of the story. Even before you use the reins, you should be telling your horse where to go by using your eyes and weight. If you look in the direction you want to go, and put a little extra weight on that side of your butt, your horse will often go without you doing anything more.

If you need to add your reins to help tell the horse what you want to do, use an 'opening' rein. Take the hand that is on the side where you want to go and move it away from the horse's neck. (Don't go too far - just an inch or two.) To go left, open your left rein. To go right, open the right one.

If the horse is looking where you want to end up, chances are his body will follow.

# Jumping Position

Jumping position is also called two-point, half-seat, or light-seat. It's a position where you stand a little bit up out of your saddle and fold forward from your hips, with bendable knees and ankles. You will end up with more weight in your legs and no weight on your butt.

Why? This position gets your weight off your horse's back and onto your legs. This helps you and your horse move in balance over jumps. Your jumping position is also good for improving your balance in the saddle, going up hills, and working over poles or cavaletti.

# Fun and Games

Here are some fun things to do on a horse that will also help your confidence and balance. You should have someone holding onto your horse before you try any of the activities. Once you can do them at the halt, have someone lead your horse while you try them at the walk or even the trot.

## Around the World:

With both feet out of your stirrup irons, take one leg over your horses neck, then the other leg over the back of your saddle. You will be facing backwards at his point, keep working your way around the horse (or the world!) until you are back where you started.

## Toe Touch:

With your feet in your stirrup irons   reach down and try to touch your right toes with your left hand, and vice-versa.

## Click Your Heels:

Take your feet out of the stirrup irons. Now, imagine your boots are ruby slippers and swing your legs up behind you to click your heels together. Give yourself bonus points if you can do it three time in a row while saying 'There's no place like home."

## Airplane:

Put both arms out to the side like you are flying, then try walking forward, standing up or getting into your jumping position without losing your balance.

# Learning to Trot

When a horse goes faster than a walk, it's a gait called 'trotting.' (What's a gait? Jump ahead to page 85 to find out.)

Trotting will feel bumpy at first, because your body will not know how to match it's movement to the movement of the horse. The first time you trot, you will usually have an instructor running beside you or be on the lunge line.

Sit tall and give a little tap with both legs. This will ask your horse for a trot. Now, as your horse moves, let your lower body wiggle with your horse like a bowl of Jello.

It will get more comfortable as you practice.

The best way to ride a trot in the beginning is learning how to 'post' (see the next page) with the beat.

## Words to Know:

Posting means moving up and down with the rhythm of your horse.

## Smart Trick:

Posting is explained on the next few pages. Turn the page to be smart.

# Posting the Trot

Posting is also called rising. It is how we move up and down in rhythm with a horse's trot.

The trot is a 'two beated' gait. That means that the horse's hooves make a '1-2' rhythm as they touch the ground.

So how do you learn to match that rhythm? Start by saying '1', '2', '1', '2', or any two-syllable word, out loud with your horse's trot. This will help you learn the rhythm of a trot.

Next, try standing on '1' and sitting on '2'. This sounds easy but takes some practice. Unless you're a super-genius at riding, you won't get it the first time. Or even in the first lesson

Sometimes it will be easier to get into a jumping position and practice touching the saddle with your seat on '1' and getting back into jumping position with '2'.

Either way, learning how to post takes patience and practice.

# Posting Diagonals

Once you can post, you can start to think about which pair of your horse's legs you are posting with. Horses move their legs in diagonal pairs when they are trotting.

You can be out of the saddle when the right front leg is swinging forward or when the left front leg is swinging forward. If you're out of the saddle when the left leg is forward, you're posting on the left diagonal.

**Words to Know:**

Diagonal pairs are named after the front foot on one side and the rear foot on the opposite side. Thus, the left front and right hind leg are the left diagonal pair.

# Switching Your Posting Diagonals

Sometimes you need to switch your posting diagonals. How do you do it?

You stick to the saddle for an extra beat. Sometimes your instructor will say 'double sit.' If you were counting out loud it would sound like this. '1', '2', '1', *'2'*, *'2'*, '1', '2'. The 1's are when you are up and the 2's are when you are sitting; the two 2's in a row are the double sit.

In an arena, we post with the outside diagonal. This helps our horse stay balanced around corners.

This rhyme will help you figure out if you are on the correct diagonal: 'rise and fall with the leg near the wall.'

# Part IX: A Few Advanced Ideas

Now that you have covered the basics, this section will show you some more advanced types of riding lessons and some of the finer points of riding.

# Gaits

What's a gait? One way to understand a gait is to think about the difference between walking and running for people. When you run, it's not just a fast walk; your whole body's movement changes to go with the faster gait.

People have two gaits: walking and running. Both human gaits have two beats, since we have two legs.

Most horses have four gaits:

**Walk:** Has four beats. The slowest, most relaxed way horses move.

**Trot:** Has two beats. The legs move in diagonal pairs, similar to when you swing your arms and skip.

**Canter:** Has three beats. Feels a bit more like being on a rocking horse, the fastest gait used in the arena.

**Gallop:** Has four beats. Very fast reserved for very experienced riders in wide open spaces, or on race tracks.

> ## Words to Know:
> The 'beat of the gait' refers to the rhythm of the horse's hooves on the ground, like the beat of music. In a canter, for example, a horse's hooves touch the ground in a '1-2-3' rhythm; a canter is a 'three beat' gait.

# Riding Lesson Topics

What things do you do in a riding lesson? What are some of the words and phrases you might hear?

**Flat Work:** Riding in an arena or level field, working on the basics, but not jumping.

**Cavaletti:** A pole connected to 'x' or square ends that you can use as a very small jump or as a ground pole. You can walk, trot or canter over cavaletti.

**Dressage:** Flat work focusing on shapes like circles and diagonals, transitions and riding in harmony with your horse.

**Games:** Fun ways to play on horseback, usually with a group. For example, you can try to carry an egg in a spoon while riding on your horse.

**Jumping:** Trotting or cantering over obstacles. Beginners usually start with very low poles, like cavaletti.

**Trail Riding:** Taking your horse for a ride through the woods or fields.

**Lunge Lessons:** Riding your horse while your instructor controls your horses speed and steering from the end of the lunge line. Good for working on your position.

> **Words to Know:**
>
> Lunge Line: Long lead used to control a horse while they travel in a circle around the instructor.

# Riding Manners

• Pass left to left. This means that if you are heading directly at another rider you should both move over a little so as you pass you could give each other a high five with you left hands.

• If you need to stop, move to the middle of the arena.

• Look out for horses that kick. Red ribbons are sometimes put in their tail at horse shows.

• Think of each horse as having a 'bubble". This bubble extends one or two horse lengths in all directions. You want to make sure you leave enough room between horses for each of them to have their own bubble.

• Listen to your instructor; they want to keep you as safe as possible.

# Part X: Finishing Up

Don't forget to put your toys away!

This part of the workbook tells you how to take good care of your horse and equipment after you ride.

# When You're Done Riding

It's nice to let your horse walk around on a long rein at the end of the ride. This means that you stay on your horse, but let the riens get a little looser, and have your horse walk for a little bit. It gives them a chance to cool down after working with you.

After that cool-down, dismount (do you remember how?), and run up your stirrup irons (do you remember that too?).

Take the reins off your horse's neck and lead him back to the barn, finding a place to tie him while you take off his tack. Usually that is the same place you used when you tacked up.

# Untacking

It's easiest to untack in reverse order of tacking up.

Start by fastening a halter around your horses neck (not their head - look at the picture).    Make sure it's attached to a cross tie or tied to a safe place.

Next, remove the bridle. Unbuckle the throatlatch and noseband, then gently slide the whole bridle off the horse's head.

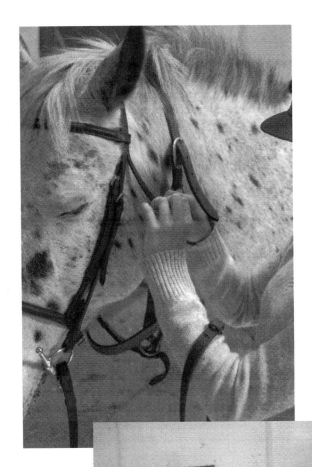

Put the halter on the horse's head and check that your horse is properly tied

Remove the saddle, starting by unbuckling your girth from both sides.  Then lift the saddle and saddle pads off.

# Cooling Down

After you have untacked your horse, check to see if they are sweaty. If they are, you will need to make sure they are cool and comfortable before you put them away.

In the Summer you can use a bucket and a sponge to clean the sweat off and cool your horse down - it's sort of like gently washing a car. You could also use a hose to run cool water over the horse's sweaty areas. Be careful when sponging or hosing around horse's head, since some horses don't like it.

In the Winter, putting a fleece or wool cooler on your horse will help them stay warm while they dry off.

If you're not sure, ask your instructor.

# Horse Treats?

Horses love a reward for their work and good behavior. Apples, carrots, and horse treats all make good snacks.

Using a bucket is the safest way to feed a treat to a horse. Using your hands is risky, since you can be accidentally bitten by your horse. To a hungry horse your fingers look a lot like carrots!

# Activity: Horse Treats

## Treat or Not?

Take a look at the things in the picture below. Which are treats for a horse? Which are not? Why?

# Putting Your Horse Away

A happy horse is a horse who has fresh water; hay or grass; a clean, dry place to take a nap; and a big hug from their rider.

Lead your horse into their stall or turnout, turn them so they are facing the door or gate, and remove their halter. Take a look to make sure they have water.

Some barns also give their horses a little hay when the horse is done working. Check with your instructor.

# Clean Your Tack

You had a fun ride.  Your horse is all tucked in and taken care of. But you have a little more work to do before you get to say you're done for the day. You have to clean your tack before you put it away.

Don't worry - it's pretty easy.

**Bridle:** Rinse the bit in some clean water.  Make sure that any hay or horse slobber(!) is cleaned off.  Wipe any sweat or dirt of the bridle with a sponge.

**Saddle:** Use a damp sponge to wipe any dust or dirt off of the saddle.

**Girth:** Clean sweat and hair off of your girth, using a sponge or brush.

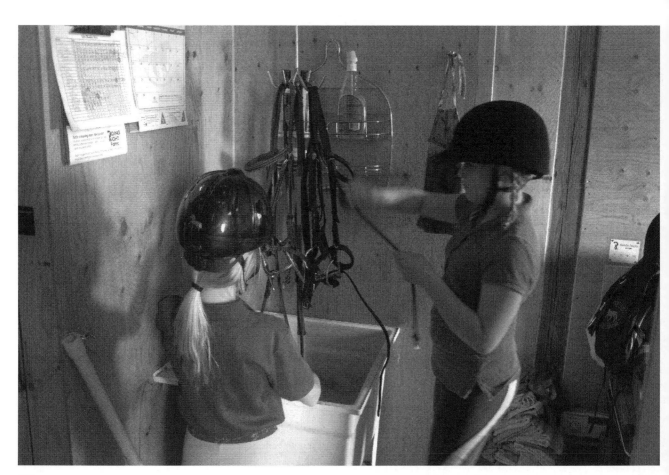

# Horse Poop Scoop

It's not over until the last poop ball is picked up!

Did your horse poop where you had them tied? Or in the arena? If so it's pooper scooper time!

Take a manure fork or shovel and scoop the poop into a manure bucket.

# Thank Your People

Don't forget to thank the people who helped with your ride!  Did your Mom, Dad, Grandma, friend, neighbor, babysitter or somebody else give you a ride to the barn?  Don't forget to say thanks to them.

The same is true for your instructor and for anybody else who gave you a hand.    Being appreciative is part of being a good rider, too.

# Answers for Activities

Horses are not like math; there is often more than one answer.  But if you're looking for hints or answers to the questions and activites, here's the place:

Standing Guard - p.2:  The horse on the right of the picture is standing guard. Notice how his ears are forward.

I'm Boss - p.3:  The boss horse is pinning his ears and pushing the other horse away from the food.

Perfect Day - p.5:  Eating, eating, eating! Wild horses spend 2/3rds of their day grazing.

Which Place - p.6: The trailer is scarier to a horse.  Any confined space worries a horse more.  The open field feels safest.

Horse's Ears - p.8: The horse on left is listening to something in front of him.  The middle horse is pinning his ears.  The horse on right is listening to something on his left.

Communication - p.9: Just like horses, people use hugs, handshakes, and other touching to communicate affection.

Horse Sense - p.11:  There are lots of similarities, so no one answer is right, but here are some examples: people and horse both turn their heads to hear better.  People shake hands and give hugs; horse will nibble gently on another horse's withers (touching). People and horses both enjoy familiar smells, such as the smell of home (or their home barn). People and horses notice the body language of others as a way of knowing who is mad, happy, scared, etc.

Happy Horses - p.15: Horses are happy doing different things at different times, but usually like being with people and other horses.

Horse Parts and People Parts - p.21: There are lots of matches, ranging from the head, eyes and ears, back to the stifle (horse) and knee (people) similarities.

Match the Horse - p.29: Black with blaze and socks is on the bottom. Bay with four pasterns and a star is on top. Paint is in the middle.

Dress to Ride - p.34: The johdpurs, gloves and helmet are good for riding.

Busy Barn - p.37: Don't forget veterinarians, stable hands, barn managers, hay suppliers, etc.

Who Are You Riding - p.38: Temperament, gaits, color, familiarity, and lots of other factors can make a horse a favorite. Reasons to ride a different horse include injury, the need for rest for the horse, different skills (such as jumping or trail work), improving the rider's variety of experience, and others.

Leading a Horse - p.43: **Not wearing a helmet.** Leading from the wrong side. Only holding rope in one hand. Rope is dragging on ground.

Grooming Tools - p.52: Curry comb, upper left: use on whole body except bony parts & face. Hoof pick, upper right: use to pick feet. Soft brush, lower left: use on whole body. Hard brush, lower right: use on whole body.

Tacking Up - p.56: The bridle, girth, and saddle pad are used to tack up.

Good Reins - p.71: Top picture - reins are too long.  Middle picture - reins are too short.  Bottom picture - reins are correct length.

Horse Treats - p.94: The apple and carrot are the best treats.  At our farm, we have one pony who likes soda from the can - but that's not common!

Made in the USA
Lexington, KY
26 July 2019